Dear Parent:
Your child's love of reading starts here

Every child learns to read in a different ~~way~~ ~~and at~~ ~~his or her own sp~~eed.
You can help your young reader improv~~e~~ ~~and build confidence~~
by encouraging his or her own interests ~~and abilities. You can also~~ guide
your child's spiritual development by rea~~ding sto~~ries with biblical values
and Bible stories, like I Can Read! books published by Zonderkidz. From
books your child reads with you to the first books he or she reads alone,
there are I Can Read! books for every stage of reading:

SHARED READING
Basic language, word repetition, and whimsical
illustrations, ideal for sharing with your emergent reader.

BEGINNING READING
Short sentences, familiar words, and simple concepts for
children eager to read on their own.

READING WITH HELP
Engaging stories, longer sentences, and language play
for developing readers.

READING ALONE
Complex plots, challenging vocabulary, and high-interest
topics for the independent reader.

ADVANCED READING
Short paragraphs, chapters, and exciting themes for the
perfect bridge to chapter books.

I Can Read! books have introduced children to the joy of reading since
1957. Featuring award-winning authors and illustrators and a fabulous
cast of beloved characters, I Can Read! books set the standard for
beginning readers.

A lifetime of discovery begins with the magical words **"I Can Read!"**

Visit www.icanread.com for information on enriching your child's reading experience.
Visit www.zonderkidz.com for more Zonderkidz I Can Read! titles.

"It's true! The LORD has risen!"
—Luke 24:34

ZONDERKIDZ

Jesus, God's Only Son

Copyright © 2010 by Zondervan
Illustrations © 2010 by Dennis G. Jones

Requests for information should be addressed to:

Zonderkidz, *Grand Rapids, Michigan 49530*

Library of Congress Cataloging-in-Publication Data

Jesus, God's only Son / pictures by Dennis G. Jones.
   p. cm. — (I can read!) (Dennis Jones series)
  ISBN 978-0-310-71880-2 (softcover)
  1. Easter—Juvenile literature. 2. Jesus Christ—Passion—Juvenile literature. 3. Jesus
Christ—Resurrection—Juvenile literature. I. Jones, Dennis G., 1956-
  BV55.J39 2010
  232.9'7—dc22   2009021966

Published in association with the literary agency of Alive Communications, Inc., 7680 Goddard Street #200, Colorado Springs, CO 80920. www.alivecommunications.com

Zonderkidz is a trademark of Zondervan. Zonderkidz is a trademark of Zondervan.

Editor: Mary Hassinger
Art direction: Sarah Molegraaf

Printed in the United States of America

14 15 LP/WOR 10 9 8 7

 ZONDERkidz

I Can Read!™

READING 2 WITH HELP

JESUS
God's Only Son

pictures by Dennis G. Jones

God's son Jesus was working hard.

Jesus wanted some time alone.

He went to a special garden

and found a quiet place to pray.

4

"God, I will do what you want
me to do," said Jesus.

Jesus heard a sound behind him.

He knew it wasn't his friends.

It was a crowd with swords and clubs.

Jesus' friend Judas was leading them.

Judas was there to trick Jesus.

He kissed Jesus and said, "Teacher."

Now the soldiers knew who Jesus was.

A soldier tied Jesus' hands together.

Jesus was calm because he knew

God was with him.

The crowd took Jesus away.

The soldiers hurt Jesus.

They made him carry a heavy cross.

"What can we do to help?"

his friends asked.

The soldiers put Jesus

on the cross.

Jesus stayed there until he died.

Jesus' friends took his body

down from the cross.

They wrapped his body

in linen cloth.

A friend carried Jesus away.

Friends buried Jesus in a cave.

A stone covered the cave door.

Jesus' friends were sad.

They thought they would

never see Jesus again.

Guards stood in front of the cave.

One morning, three women
went to the cave.

They brought spices for Jesus.

The stone that covered the cave
was rolled away.

The guards were gone.

The cave was empty!

"Where could Jesus be?"

one of the women asked.

"Did someone steal his body?"

An angel sat by the cave.

"I know you are looking for Jesus.

He has risen, just like he said.

Go tell his friends,"

said the angel.

Then a man walked up to the women.

"Do not be afraid," he said.

The women were amazed.

The man was Jesus.

He had been dead,

but now he was alive.

"Go tell my friends to meet me,"

said Jesus.

Jesus met his friends.

They were happy to see him.

Jesus said he had to go to heaven.

"Tell everyone about God," he said.

Then Jesus went up to heaven.

Jesus is watching over you.
Someday you will meet him
in heaven.